BEAUTIFUL DOGS

PORTRAITS

of

CLASSIC
BREEDS

BEAUTIFUL DOGS

PORTRAITS

of

CLASSIC BREEDS

by CAROLYN MENTEITH
photographed by ANDREW PERRIS

Ivy Press

First published in the UK in 2013 by

Ivy Press

210 High Street

Lewes

East Sussex BN7 2NS

United Kingdom

www.ivypress.co.uk

British Library Cataloguing-in-Publication Data

A catalogue record for this book is available from the British Library

ISBN: 978-1-78240-075-2

This book was conceived, designed and produced by

Ivy Press

Creative Director Peter Bridgewater

Publisher Susan Kelly

Editorial Director Tom Kitch

Art Director James Lawrence

Designer Ginny Zeal

Photographer Andrew Perris

Illustrator David Anstey

Printed in China

Colour origination by Ivy Press Reprographics

10 9 8 7 6 5 4 3 2 1

Distributed worldwide (except North America) by Thames & Hudson Ltd, 181A High Holborn, London WC1V 7QX, United Kingdom

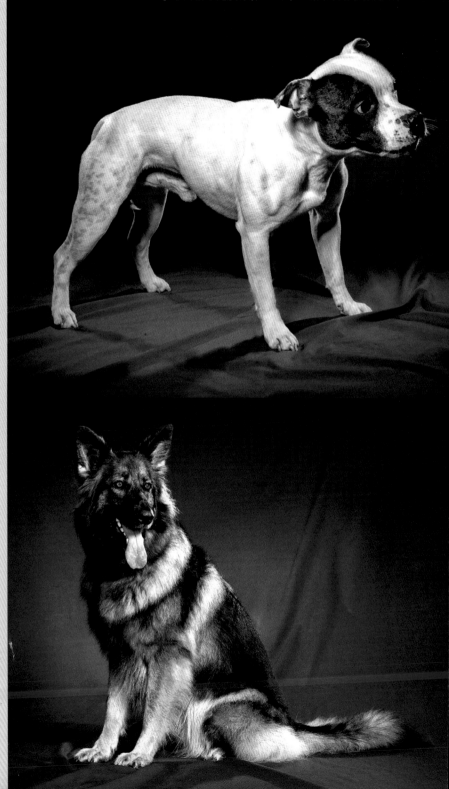

CONTENTS

INTRODUCTION

FOR OVER FIFTEEN THOUSAND YEARS, DOGS HAVE been invaluable companions to humans. They have played a fundamental part in the growth of our civilization, and as a result have earned the title of 'man's best friend'. No other two species share the relationship that dogs and humans have. This symbiotic partnership has covered everything from providing friendship to working together, whether that work might be hunting, herding, guarding or any one of a whole host of other tasks where the dog has proved its worth.

Their versatility has led to them still playing a vital role in modern life. As the traditional jobs that dogs have performed have died out, they have adapted to modern life and new roles. They work as assistance dogs for the disabled, search out explosives, drugs or missing persons, give warning of impending seizures and even detect some forms of cancer. Dogs can and often do save lives.

In *Beautiful Dogs*, we celebrate dogs in a few of their numerous forms. Some of the dogs presented here are champion show dogs, while others are much-loved companions. Each photo-

Above: Humans and dogs have worked side-by-side for thousands of years, a special relationship that continues to this day

graph shows a different breed, developed in the past by humans or by circumstances to do a specific job – and now, with the advent of the show ring, to have a particular appearance.

Each dog featured in the book comes with a description of the breed's history, where it originated and what it was originally bred to do. Nowadays, most purebred dogs are bred for the show ring or, far more often, as companions and family dogs. In many cases, their working relatives still continue in their original roles, but few of these find their way into the world of dog shows.

To fully appreciate the beauty of dogs, you need to see how they move, discover their personalities and share their enthusiasm for life in order to understand just why they hold such a special place in so many people's hearts and lives – and I hope this book will inspire you to do just that.

Enjoy discovering in this book a small sample of the world's many varied dog breeds – from the common to the rare, from the hunter to the companion, from the silky to the dreadlocked – but all of them beautiful.

THE DEVELOPMENT OF THE DOG

THE DOMESTIC DOG – CANIS LUPUS FAMILIARIS – IS a member of the Canidae family, which also includes wolves, foxes, coyotes and jackals. The term 'domestic dog' refers to both the domesticated and the feral varieties of the species. While we may think of the dog as a pet, the vast majority of the world's dog population comprises feral or street dogs.

The development of the dog from its wild, canid ancestors, most notably the wolf, is an incredible evolutionary success story – reflected by the fact that there are only around 400,000 wolves left in the world but an incredible 400,000,000 dogs.

Although it can be argued that humans are responsible for the wolf's demise by encroaching on its territory, the wolf as a species has been less able to adapt to change, and any alteration in its environment produces a drop in the population. The dog, however, developed as a true expert at finding and exploiting the niches created by humans.

The separation of dogs from wolves and wild canids happened around 15,000 years ago, when humans stopped being nomadic and began to live in settlements. Up until then, these animals had avoided humans but some discovered that with the new settlements came a valuable food resource – human rubbish dumps.

However, it was only the less fearful wolves and wild canids that were able to exploit this new resource, and who became the fittest to pass on their genes to the next generation. With only 5 to 10% of a wild population's puppies surviving to adulthood, it was only the tamer individuals that prospered in this new environment.

In what evolutionarily was a very short time, these new canids were so desensitised to man, and the benefits in terms of resources were so huge, that they moved inside the settlements. They were encouraged to do so by humans who realised that the animals could give early warning of approaching predators, and also their eating of waste kept the settlements clean and vermin free. In periods of famine, they were also used as food.

This newly developed animal was to be the genetic link between the wolf and the huge range of current dog breeds around today.

Above: Dogs have evolved to be social and share our lives, and today our 'best friend' provides both loyal friendship and protection

THE DEVELOPMENT OF BREEDS

THERE IS AN INCREDIBLY LARGE RANGE OF SHAPES and sizes of dogs. It seems extraordinary that a Chihuahua and a Great Dane could even be the same species. Not only are different breeds and types very varied physically, but they have also become highly specialised due to centuries of selective breeding.

To understand how successfully dogs have developed, you only need compare them with their ancestor, the wolf, and you will find there is a breed that can outperform it. For example, Siberian Huskies can run further, Greyhounds can run faster, Bloodhounds can follow scent more effectively and Borzois can see better.

While it is thought that dogs domesticated themselves, when it comes to the development of breeds, humans played the starring role. We worked out early on in our relationship with dogs that there were some jobs that dogs were perfect for, whether it was guarding, herding, retrieving or hunting.

A dog's ability to do these jobs came from a sequence of behaviours that its ancestors used to gather food, which is, or at least was, hard-wired in every dog. This hunting motor pattern can be broken down into the following stages: 'eye' (see the prey); stalk; chase; grab/bite (grab the prey); kill/bite (kill the prey); and dissect/eat.

To develop the dogs that were needed to perform various tasks, humans started to breed dogs to develop these motor pattern abilities. Herding dogs, for example, needed to be good at the first part (eye–stalk–chase) but not the second (grab/bite–kill/bite–dissect/eat), i.e. able to move the sheep but not kill them.

Therefore dogs that were really good at only certain parts of the motor pattern were bred with other dogs that also showed strengths and weaknesses in those specific areas to produce specialized breeds.

Above: Bloodhounds (noble, 'blooded hounds') are among the oldest breed of dog that hunt by scent, and are both trackers and companions

A by-product of breeding for working ability was that different forms of dog began to emerge that were physically best able to do that job. Not only that, but the area of the world they developed in also played a vital role. For example, the further away from the equator the dogs were, the larger they tended to be, as they needed a bigger body with more protection around the vital organs to withstand extreme cold.

FROM WORKING DOG TO SHOW RING

WHILE THE LIFE OF A SHOW DOG IS VERY different to that of a working dog, show dogs are split into groups that correspond to those original working functions. While the groups vary in different countries, the method of judging is more or less the same.

First of all, a dog will compete against other members of its breed, age, experience and sex. The winner of each of those classes will go on to compete for the Best Dog or Best Bitch. Then the Best Dog and Bitch will compete against each other to determine the Best of Breed. These winners then go on to compete in the Best of Group competition and, if successful, Best in Show.

For the Kennel Club and the American Kennel Club (AKC), these groups are:

Working – these are largely the guard dogs, whether guarding people, property or livestock. They also include the sledge dogs.

Pastoral (Herding in AKC) – these are the herding dogs that work with shepherds and farmers to move livestock.

Hound – these hunting dogs are split into scent hounds and sight hounds.

Above: Sheepdogs are hard-working dogs; some will work alone, while others, as shown here, will work as part of a team

Terrier – these are the vermin killers developed to work in different areas and conditions.

Toy – these are small dogs, historically bred mostly for rich ladies, although some have monastic origins.

Gun dog (Sporting in AKC) – these dogs have been developed for working to the gun and are split into four main types: retrievers, spaniels, pointers and HPR (hunt, point and retrieve).

Utility (Non-Sporting in AKC) – these are the dogs that don't easily fit in any other group.

The Fédération Cynologique Internationale (FCI), an international federation of 87 kennel clubs, has quite different groups, however (and many more breeds). They include sheepdogs and cattle dogs; pinscher and schnauzer, molossoid and Swiss mountain dogs; terriers; dachshunds; and spitz and primitive types.

Pointers and setters are in the same group and the retrievers category includes flushing dogs and water dogs. There is also a section for companion and toy dogs, and scent hounds and related breeds are a separate group from sight hounds.

THE HISTORY OF DOG SHOWS

DOG SHOWS HAVE BEEN GOING ON FOR CENTURIES but until fairly recently they have been very different from the Crufts-type shows that we are familiar with nowadays. Throughout history, the Egyptians, Greeks, Romans, Celts, Bedouin, Afghans, French, Australians, Russians, and even the British, have all had shows where they decorated, showed off and then raced their sight hounds with great pomp and ceremony.

Terrier men also held competitions where they would exhibit their finest dogs in tip-top condition – and then test the dogs to see which could kill the most rats. In other words, dog shows were about what a dog could do and not how it looked. Today these displays of usefulness and working ability have changed into displays of canine beauty.

The man who bears much of the responsibility for that was the young entrepreneur Charles Cruft, who, in 1886, organised a dog show in London. Billed as the 'First Great Terrier Show', the show had 57 classes and 600 entries – but was just for terriers. In 1891, however, when 'Cruft's Greatest Dog Show' was held at the Royal Agricultural Hall in London, it was the first show at which all breeds were invited to compete, and around 2,000 dogs participated at this inaugural show.

As a result, by the end of the nineteenth century, dog shows were changing. What had once been a competition of working ability, had transformed into the appearance-driven shows that we now recognise – and breeding and showing purebred dogs had become a major recreational activity in many parts of the world.

In the US, this also took place at the Westminster Dog Show, which was set up in 1877 – and has been running in one form or another ever since – making it the second-longest running sporting event in America (the Kentucky Derby is the longest).

And the Fédération Cynologique Internationale (FCI), an organisation that has 87 individual member countries, runs the World Dog Show, which is held in a different country each year.

When Charles Cruft died in 1938, his widow asked the Kennel Club to take his show over. In 1948 the very first Crufts Dog Show was organized by the Kennel Club – which runs it to this day.

Above: Stingray of Derryabah, a British Lakeland Terrier, wins Best in Show at the 92nd Westminster Kennel Club show in 1968

SHOWS TODAY

Since 1965, dogs have had to qualify to enter Crufts. The idea was suggested in order to limit the number of entries. In order to qualify to compete at Crufts, the dogs have to have won a prize at a championship show in the preceding year. This means that being able to describe a dog as 'qualified for Crufts' is an accolade in itself. Crufts is still the world's largest dog show with around 28,000 dogs competing in the showing classes each year.

The Westminster Kennel Club Dog Show is run on slightly different lines to many other shows, as the shortage of space at Madison Square Gardens in New York where the show is held means it can only take 2,500 entries. Those are filled immediately on the day entries are accepted with only champions being allowed to compete – although there are plans to change this.

The dog that wins overall becomes 'America's Dog' for the next year and starts a media tour that will see it appearing on virtually every TV network. It even visits the observation deck of the Empire State Building,

which lights its tower purple and gold – the Westminster colours – during the show in tribute. The Westminster Dog Show was also made famous in Christopher Guest's comedy film *Best in Show*, with the fictional Mayflower Dog Show being very obviously based on Westminster.

The FCI's World Dog Show first appeared on the dog show calendar in 1971. It was held in Budapest, Hungary, for just a few hundred entrants. Since then, it has been held in a different country each year and now attracts around 20,000 entries.

Whether competing at Crufts, Westminster or the World Dog Show, to walk away with the title of Best in Show is the pinnacle of canine achievement – and for many owners, it is the culmination of a lifetime of hard work. Years of breeding, months of preparation and sometimes weeks of grooming will all culminate in a few minutes in the ring – where for a select few, canine dreams of glory come true, or else are shattered with the dismissive wave of a judge's hand. However, it is important to remember the old adage, 'win or lose, you always take the best dog home'.

Above: Each year around 28,000 dogs attend the Crufts Dog Show, a hugely popular, four-day event held in Birmingham, in central England

WHAT IS THE JUDGE LOOKING FOR?

For those people who watch dog shows, especially group judging, many have clear ideas about which dog they want to win. It may be the same breed as their own dog, or it may have the look they prefer – whether that is sleek and elegant, shaggy and scruffy, large and loveable or small and endearing. When the judges eventually make their selection, observers are often astonished as to why on earth they chose 'that dog!', which can be the cause of some heated debate among spectators.

For the judges standing in the ring, however, their job is not to choose the one that appeals to them the most. Their job is to first make sure the dog is healthy and 'fit for function', after which they are comparing each dog to the canine blueprint – the breed standard.

This standard – which may vary slightly in each country – describes the most perfect example of the breed, and so what the judge is looking for is the dog that is the closest to its breed standard in every possible way.

The breed standard will tell the judge what size the dog should be, what kind of

Above: Judges compare each entry to the breed standard, watching the dog move and using their hands to assess form to reach a decision

coat it should have, what colours are permitted or are desirable in the breed, and some very detailed descriptions of the physical appearance. In many cases the breed standard will also describe the ideal personality that the breed should possess.

To understand what it is that a judge is looking for and why sometimes the decisions made can seem strange, it is perhaps best to get a view from one of them.

As one top show judge explains, the importance of matching the breed standard cannot be overestimated. They consider the breed standard as cast in stone and it is their bible, 'to be observed as if you were a canine fundamentalist'. Of course in reality they can't judge a dog with a tape measure and a set of scales so they have to develop a picture of what they think the perfect dog and the perfect type is.

But it is important to grasp that knowing the breed standard and understanding the breed standard are two completely different things… In the words of one show judge: 'I mean just because you know your times tables doesn't make you a mathematician does it?'.

THE DOGS

This GORGEOUS GALLERY of *dog diversity* and *canine charm* will FASCINATE, INTRIGUE and DELIGHT any fancier. *Take a leisurely stroll* along our carefully selected, BEAUTIFULLY PHOTOGRAPHED dog walk and encounter over forty breeds, each one boasting its own *unique features* and *abilities*. It will certainly put a springer in your step.

PAPILLON

BITCH

The large, butterfly-type ears give this dog its name, as 'papillon' is French for 'butterfly'. A surprisingly hardy dog for its size, it has been one of the most popular toy breeds in continental Europe for over 200 years, combining beauty and brains in a small package. The PAPILLON was very much a high-status dog, popular in the royal courts of Europe and owned by both Marie Antoinette and Madame Pompadour.

Features

With its alert expression, round, dark eyes, long, silky, fine coat, beautiful markings and trademark butterfly ears, this is a lovely looking dog that makes an ideal companion. The Papillon has small, dainty, hare-like feet with tufts of hair between its toes, and a plumed tail that arches over its back. It is mostly white with patches, or tricoloured.

Use

Papillons have found work in all kinds of different areas, including assisting deaf people by alerting their owners to sounds such as doorbells and fire alarms. As well as being companion dogs, they also often compete in mini-agility and obedience.

Similar breeds

Long-coated Chihuahua, Japanese Chin

Height

Dog .... 23–28 cm (9–11 in)

Bitch ..... 20–25.5 cm (8–10 in)

Origin

The breed was developed in Belgium in the eighteenth century as an erect-eared version of the Phàlene (French for 'moth') – a popular breed dating back to the thirteenth century. Now the Papillon is by far the more popular, and while the Phàlene still exists, both breeds are now shown together as Papillons.

Belgium

AFGHAN HOUND

DOG

The Afghan Hound has been highly prized by the nomads of Afghanistan for centuries. While these dogs may look like supermodels, they were bred to hunt hares, foxes, deer, gazelle, jackals, wolves and even leopards. With their keen eyesight, Afghan Hounds would run fearlessly and tirelessly ahead of mounted hunters in the pursuit of their prey.

Features

This breed is probably one of the most elegant and spectacular of all the hounds, with its aristocratically long nose, almond-shaped eyes, level back, pronounced hip bones, curved tail and very long, flowing, fine coat. The Afghan Hound can be any colour.

Use

Afghan Hounds are free spirits but despite this, they make good companions because they are affectionate to their owners. They also tolerate children well, aren't above playing the clown, and are playful with other dogs. In a recent study of the most intelligent dog breeds, Afghans came at the bottom. This doesn't necessarily mean that they are stupid – just that they see no point in training! They are also occasionally used for hound racing.

Similar breeds

Borzoi, Saluki

Height

Dog .... 66–71 cm (26–28 in)

Bitch ..... 61–66 cm (24–26 in)

Origin

These dogs were highly prized in their home country of Afghanistan and indeed, every year, they were brought down from the mountains by their nomadic owners for a special festival at which they were the guests of honour and were dressed in traditional necklaces and flowers.

Afghanistan

POINTER

BITCH

This breed is a very specialized gun dog that gets its name from its job – when hunting, the POINTER sniffs the air with its head held high as it scans the area until its keen nose scents prey. Then it slows to a halt, pointing like an arrow at the vital spot to allow the hunters to approach and flush the game for the guns.

Features

The Pointer gives an instant impression of both power and grace. It has a noble head, dark, round eyes, long, straight legs, a tapering tail and oval feet with well-arched toes. Its coat is short and dense to keep it weatherproof and it can be lemon and white, orange and white, liver and white, and black and white, as well as self coloured and tricoloured.

Use

Pointers are still used in the field as working gun dogs although not in large numbers. The breed has an even temperament and is fairly calm and sensitive, making it a good family dog and companion breed, as long as it gets plenty of exercise.

Similar breeds

German Pointer, Hungarian Vizsla

Height

Dog .... 64–69 cm (25–27 in)

Bitch ..... 61–66 cm (24–26 in)

Origin

The Pointer is a racy-looking dog that first appeared in England around 1650 – most likely as a result of crossing Greyhounds, Foxhounds and Bloodhounds with some sort of spaniel! It may also have some Spanish blood.

England

BEDLINGTON TERRIER

DOG

The BEDLINGTON TERRIER, while looking like a docile lamb when groomed for the show ring, is very much a terrier at heart with a working history of hunting vermin. This breed was also raced for sport as its body shape (and the Whippet in its ancestry) means that this is a fast dog with great endurance and stamina.

Features

This is a graceful, lithe dog with a characteristically narrow, pear-shaped head. It has a deep chest and a natural arch to its back, which creates a tucked-up underline. It has long, hare-like feet and a moderate-length tail that tapers to a point, and while gracefully curved doesn't come over its back. The Bedlington's thick, linty coat stands out from the skin and can be blue, liver or sandy, with or without tan. It needs regular trimming to keep it in its proper form.

Use

The Bedlington has a gentle temperament and makes an energetic family dog and good companion. This breed is sometimes crossed with larger hounds to produce a medium-sized Lurcher.

Similar breeds

Miniature Poodle, Lagotto Romangnolo

Height

Dog .... 41–43 cm (16–17 in)

Bitch ..... 38–41 cm (15–16 in)

Origin

The breed is named after the mining area of Northumberland in England where it was developed and became popular in the mid-nineteenth century. Its ancestor was the now non-existent vermin-catching Rothbury Terrier, which was then crossed with the Whippet for extra speed, and also quite possibly the Dandie Dinmont Terrier.

England

STAFFORDSHIRE BULL TERRIER

DOG

Originally developed in the second half of the nineteenth century as a fighting dog, the STAFFORDSHIRE BULL TERRIER was designed to combine the muscle power of the Bulldog with the intelligence and agility of a terrier. Despite this link, the breed has developed and gone on to be one of the most popular companion dogs in the UK.

Features

The Staffordshire Bull Terrier is a muscular, active dog whose distinctive face with pronounced cheek muscles and a wide mouth, gives it the typical Stafford grin. It has a level back, wide front and should be well defined and muscular. The tail looks like an old-fashioned pump handle. The coat can be a variety of colours – red, fawn, white, black, blue, or any of these colours with white. It can also be any shade of brindle with white.

Use

While it isn't always good with other dogs without a lot of early and ongoing socialization, this tough, fun and affectionate breed is a good companion dog – friendly and outgoing with people, and excellent with children.

Similar breeds

Bull Terrier, Bulldog

Height

Dog .... 38–41 cm (15–16 in)

Bitch ..... 35.5–38 cm (14–15 in)

Origin

Developed originally by James Hinks of Birmingham, England, this breed was appearing at dog shows as early as 1862. It wasn't until the 1930s, however, that it was recognized as being a separate breed from the Bull Terrier, and it had a name change to distinguish the two, adding the county name where it had become so popular.

England

BOLOGNESE
DOG

This toy dog has a history stretching back to at least the eleventh century, where the breed was the choice of many European aristocrats. Despite this, the BOLOGNESE is still a fairly rare breed and it didn't appear in the USA at all until the 1980s. Unlike many long-coated dogs, this breed doesn't have an undercoat as it was bred to cope in a hot climate.

Features

The Bolognese is a square, compact toy dog with a long, flocked coat without curl that covers the entire head and body. The ears are set high and carried away from the head, giving it a broad appearance. The tail is well-feathered and carried curved over its back. Its lips, eyelids, nose and nails are black while the coat is always white.

Use

These dogs are still the companions that they have been throughout their history – and their intelligent, friendly nature coupled with their appealing look wins them many friends wherever they go. They are, however, totally devoted to their owners, rarely leaving their side.

Similar breeds

Maltese, Coton De Tulear

Height

Dog .... 26.5–30.5 cm (10½–12 in)

Bitch ..... 25.5–28 cm (10–11 in)

Origin

The Bolognese is Italian, but given the age of this breed, its true origins are lost in the past and it may well have descended from the Maltese dog. Other accounts, however, say that it was the other way around, and that the Maltese dog is descended from the Bolognese!

Italy

GERMAN SHEPHERD DOG

BITCH

The GERMAN SHEPHERD DOG is one of the world's most popular dog breeds. The breed club was originally based in Stuttgart, then Munich, then Berlin – all areas where the breed was popular. The breed was also known as the 'Alsatian' by many kennel clubs before they reverted to the breed's original name in 1977.

Features

With upright, pointed ears, a long nose, bushy tail and thick, medium-to-long coat with a thick undercoat, this is a large, almost wolf-like dog. In some countries, the breed has been developed to have a sloping back but this is subject to controversy. The German Shepherd can be black (or black saddle) with tan or gold to light grey markings, all black, or all grey with lighter or brown markings (referred to as sables).

Use

This breed is used as a guard dog, a police and military dog, an assistance dog, as a companion and for obedience competitions. It is loyal, devoted, easily trained and truly versatile, and since it's capable of taking on just about any canine job, it is probably one of the dog world's top workers.

Similar breeds

Belgian Shepherd, Beauceron

Height

Dog .... 58–66 cm (23–26 in)

Bitch ..... 56–64 cm (22–25 in)

Origin

The breed was developed in Germany in the nineteenth century, when dogs were needed to move and control large flocks of sheep. Crosses were produced of all the working dogs in the region to eventually produce the perfect dog. Despite its wolfish appearance, the Pekingese is actually genetically closer to the wolf than the German Shepherd Dog!

Germany

FOXHOUND

DOG

Despite the large number of working Foxhounds, this is a rare dog in the show ring. In the hunting field this is a dog that pushes canine stamina to the limits, and it has been bred over hundreds of years for endurance and pack compatibility. The FOXHOUND gets on well with most other dogs, is happy and amiable towards people but its attitude to anything small and furry tends towards the lethal.

Features

The Foxhound is a solidly built dog, with straight front legs, a straight back, long neck and round, tight feet. The tail is carried jauntily over its back. The short coat can be any hound colour, but the traditional colours of white, tan and black are preferred.

Use

Their main use is for hunting foxes. Foxhounds can make companion dogs but they are a challenge as they can be active in the house, noisy (hounds do bay), are excellent escape artists and training is a mystery to them! And, of course, they are rarely safe with smaller animals so do not always mix with other pets. They are first and foremost pack hounds.

Similar breeds

Hamiltonstovare, Beagle

Height

Dog .... 64–69 cm (25–27 in)

Bitch ..... 58–64 cm (23–25 in)

Origin

The Foxhound was developed in England as a pack hound to hunt foxes in a large group, and it is a true canine specialist. The breed can be traced back to the 1700s – in fact most Foxhound pedigrees can be traced in an unbroken line back to this date, as the Master of each pack kept very careful records.

England

GERMAN SPITZ
DOG

There are two sizes of GERMAN SPITZ – the Mittel and the Klein – with no differences between the two apart from the size. The original spitz dogs from Germany were large dogs descended from the big northern breeds, but attempts to reduce their size ended up producing the diminutive Pomeranian. In the 1970s an attempt was made to reverse this process, resulting in these two sizes of 'larger Poms'.

Features

The German Spitz is a square-looking dog with small, triangular, erect ears and dark, oval-shaped eyes. Its paws are almost cat-like and the tail is covered with an abundance of hair and is carried over its back. The breed has a profuse double coat consisting of a soft, woolly undercoat and a long, harsh, straight topcoat that can be any colour and have any markings.

Use

The German Spitz is an intelligent, active dog that is utterly devoted to its family. This, coupled with its happy disposition and confident nature, makes it a fabulous companion.

Similar breeds

Pomeranian, Japanese Spitz

Height

Mittel.... 30.5–38 cm (12–15 in)

Klein ..... 23–28 cm (9–11 in)

Origin

While these dogs are the descendants of German dogs, the reversal of the miniaturization process is one that has largely been going on in the UK. The names German Spitz (Mittel) and German Spitz (Klein) are an attempt to link these breeds to their continental equivalents – the Standard German Spitz and the Miniature German Spitz.

Germany

FRENCH BULLDOG

DOG

Although its ancestors were from England, the FRENCH BULLDOG started life as a rural companion in the French countryside. However, when stories of its unconventional appearance spread to Paris, the breed was adopted by those who wanted to appear socially daring. Postcards can still sometimes be found of scantily clad women posing with their 'Bouledogues Français'.

Features

The French Bulldog is an enchanting looking little dog which has the appearance of a miniaturized but bat-eared bulldog, with the same flat face, short tail and smooth, short coat – but all in a much smaller package. Although this is a small breed, it is muscular with a heavy bone structure and strong legs. The colour of the coat can be either fawn, brindle or pied.

Use

This is a friendly, good-natured and playful dog, which makes an ideal, affectionate, fun companion or family dog. As a result of its rural and urban heritage, it is just as happy living in towns and cities as it is living in the countryside.

Similar breeds

Boston Terrier, Pug

Height

Dog .... 30.5 cm (12 in)

Bitch ..... 30.5 cm (12 in)

Origin

This breed is originally descended from the Toy Bulldog – a miniaturized version of the British Bulldog that was popular with the lace-makers of Nottingham, England. During the industrial revolution, many relocated to France with their dogs, where the breed changed, possibly with the inclusion of other breeds including the Pug and some terrier, to create the French Bulldog of today.

France

ALASKAN MALAMUTE
DOG

As well as being the largest of the Arctic sled dogs, the ALASKAN MALAMUTE is also the oldest. The breed was only discovered when Russian explorers visited Alaska in the1800s and were struck by these incredible dogs and the strong bond they had with the people of the area – often sharing their dwellings. These powerful sled dogs also worked as pack animals.

Features

The Alaskan Malamute is a heavily boned, powerfully built dog with strong, muscular legs and a deep chest. The Malamute coat is coarse with a dense undercoat and a plumed tail carried over its back. It has brown, almond-shaped eyes and small, triangular, erect ears that can be folded back when working. The Malamute ranges in colour from light grey to black, or from sable to red.

Use

These are first and foremost working dogs, although they are also used as companion dogs, for Cani-X and as racing sled dogs. While this is an affectionate, friendly breed that learns quickly, the dogs have fairly specialized requirements in terms of exercise, training and grooming.

Similar breeds

Siberian Husky, Canadian Eskimo Dog

Height

Dog .... 64–71 cm (25–28 in)

Bitch ..... 58–66 cm (23–26 in)

Origin

The Alaskan Malamute got its name from an Inuit tribe called Mahlemuts who lived in Alaska. The breed was protected from interference by outsiders for centuries – but when sled-racing became popular at the end of the 1800s, the breed was crossed with smaller, faster dogs and nearly died out. However, two US enthusiasts saved and rebuilt the breed.

USA

GRIFFON BRUXELLOIS
DOG

The GRIFFON BRUXELLOIS (or Brussels Griffon) is a toy breed that looks a bit like a cross between a workman-like terrier and a monkey! This breed has a real rags-to-riches story because its ancestors were the pest-control experts of Belgium, employed to kill the vermin in the city stables. But when 'discovered' in 1870 by the Belgian queen Henrietta Maria, the breed quickly became the dog of nobility.

Features

These small, square dogs are level in the back and have a short, wiry, harsh coat and a characteristically flat, yet cheeky face. They have large, black eyes with long eyelashes, a prominent bearded chin and an almost human expression. Their feet are round and cat-like with black nails. The coat of the Griffon Bruxellois can be red, black, brown or a rich tan in colour.

Use

The main use of this breed nowadays is as a companion dog. However, the working instincts of the Griffon Bruxellois remain, making it a playful, inquisitive and fun pet that will enjoy a good game as much, if not more, than a walk.

Similar breeds

Affenpinscher, Norfolk Terrier

Height

Dog .... 18–20 cm (7–8 in)

Bitch ..... 18–20 cm (7–8 in)

Origin

The breed was established in Belgium by crossing the Affenpinscher with Belgian street dogs (which looked a little similar to the Fox Terrier). While the Griffon Bruxellois lived mostly in the stables, during the day they could often be seen perched on cab drivers' seats around the cities, helping to establish the breed's popularity.

Belgium

MANCHESTER TERRIER

DOG

The MANCHESTER TERRIER is one of the oldest terriers in the world. Like most terriers, it was named after the area where the breed was developed, and in the city of Manchester in England in the mid 1800s, sanitation was poor and the rats were taking over. This new terrier quickly became the city's rodent catcher *par excellence.*

Features

The Manchester Terrier has black, sparkling, almond-shaped eyes, small V-shaped ears, and a long, narrow, wedge-shaped head on a slim graceful neck. The top line shows a very slight arch, and the chest is narrow with a deep brisket and a tucked-up abdomen. Legs are straight and muscular with compact feet and black nails. The Manchester Terrier is always jet black and a rich mahogany tan.

Use

These dogs are used as companions, although they still retain their hunting instincts. This is now a very rare breed that is on the Vulnerable Native Breed list in the UK, in stark contrast to earlier years when the breed was so popular that it became known as the Gentleman's Terrier.

Similar breeds

Miniature Pinscher, German Pinscher

Height

Dog .... 41 cm (16 in)

Bitch ..... 38 cm (15 in)

Origin

Developed in England, this breed was a cross between the traditional black and tan terrier of the 1800s and the whippet, which gave it its speed. While most terriers were designed as rural vermin catchers, this one was designed specifically to work in the city. The Manchester Terrier is a true terrier, despite looking like a miniature Dobermann.

England

HUNGARIAN PULI

BITCH

With a heavy, corded coat, the HUNGARIAN PULI is one of the more unusual dogs to look at. The shepherds who worked on the plains of Hungary would generally use these dogs in tandem with other flock-guarding breeds such as the similarly corded Komondor. Working Pulis would have their coats clipped each summer at the same time as the sheep.

Features

This is a sturdy, muscular dog that should look square when viewed from the side. Under the covering of hair, it has a small, fine head with medium-sized, dark brown eyes. The ears are V-shaped and about half the length of its head. The most striking characteristic is the profuse corded coat, looking like dreadlocks, in either black, black with grey, grey or fawn. It is virtually waterproof and protects the dog from harsh weather.

Use

This is a nimble and intelligent breed that tends to be wary of strangers, but is used mostly as a companion dog. There is no reason (apart from its restrictive coat) why it couldn't work in agility or obedience.

Similar breeds

Bergamasco, Komondor

Height

Dog .... 41–44 cm (16–17½ in)

Bitch ..... 37–41 cm (14½–16 in)

Origin

This is an ancient breed that has been used to herd sheep on the Hungarian plains since at least the ninth century, and it has remained pure for centuries. It is thought that the ancestors of these dogs arrived from the East and may be the same stock that produced the Tibetan Terrier.

Hungary

GOLDEN RETRIEVER
BITCH

The GOLDEN RETRIEVER is one of the most popular companion dogs in the world. The breed was established in Scotland in the early 1900s and was first registered with the Kennel Club in 1903, although it didn't make its way to the USA until much later, being registered in 1932. The breed was established with the aim of creating the ideal gun dog, predominantly to retrieve waterfowl.

Features

This medium- to large-sized dog is recognizable first for its flat or wavy golden coat with feathering on the legs and tail. It has a broad skull, dark brown eyes, a balanced, short coupled body with a level top line, and strong legs. It moves powerfully with good drive, and can be any shade of gold or cream.

Use

Easily trainable, friendly to all and keen to please, the Golden Retriever is an excellent family dog and can also be found doing all kinds of jobs including disability assistance, search and rescue, working trials, obedience and agility training, as well as its original job as a working game retriever.

Similar breeds

Labrador Retriever, Flat-coated Retriever

Height

Dog .... 56–61 cm (22–24 in)

Bitch ..... 51–56 cm (20–22 in)

Origin

This breed was established on Lord Tweedmouth's estate at Guisachan, near Inverness in Scotland using a Flat-coated Retriever, Tweed Water Spaniel and an Irish Setter, after he had purchased the only yellow puppy from a litter of black Wavy-coated Retrievers belonging to a Brighton cobbler (although some accounts say from a Brighton circus!).

Scotland

NORFOLK TERRIER

DOG

The Norfolk Terrier is a fairly new breed that was only recognized in the UK in 1964 and the USA in 1979. Up until then, these dogs with their folded ears were classed along with the prick-eared versions as Norwich Terriers. It was only when breeders started to breed them separately to avoid odd ears from breeding one to the other, that the breed was given its own name.

Features

The Norfolk Terrier is one of the smallest of the terriers but is compact and strong with good substance. It has a broad, wedge-shaped head, oval-shaped eyes that are either dark brown or black and V-shaped ears that drop forward close to its cheek. The coat is hard, wiry and straight and can be all shades of red, wheaten, black and tan, or grizzle.

Use

Unlike some terriers, Norfolks have a loveable, easy-going disposition, which make them a great family and companion dog. Their folding ears make them look softer than their close relative, the Norwich Terrier, and, to many people, more appealing. They can also be seen competing in mini-agility.

Similar breeds

Norwich Terrier, Cairn Terrier

Height

Dog .... 25.5 cm (10 in)

Bitch ..... 23 cm (9 in)

Origin

The origins of this breed began at Cambridge University in England in the 1870s when it was fashionable among the undergraduates to own a terrier. These dogs were obtained from a livery stable that existed near the colleges – one was given to the owner of a stable yard near Norwich and became the founder of this new breed.

England

AMERICAN COCKER SPANIEL
BITCH

The AMERICAN COCKER SPANIEL is the smallest of the gun dog group in the UK and the sporting group in the USA. An argument rages, however, as to whether the English or American breed is the 'real' Cocker Spaniel. In the USA, this breed is referred to as the Cocker Spaniel, while the UK version is the 'English Cocker Spaniel'. In the UK, however, the reverse is true!

Features

This breed is a smaller, showier version of its English cousin, and while it has a shorter nose and a more domed head, they both share the same long ears, heavily feathered body, and silky, medium-to-long length coat. The American Cocker can be black, black with tan points, buff, red or chocolate and can also have white markings.

Use

Their main use is as companion dogs as they are a pleasure to train and can excel at anything they put their mind mind to – including obedience and heelwork to music, but despite their merry nature, they can be rather stubborn! They do make an ideal family dog, being affectionate with all the family.

Similar breeds

English Cocker Spaniel, Cavalier King Charles Spaniel

Height

Dog .... 35.5–40 cm (14–15½ in)

Bitch ..... 34–38 cm (13½–15 in)

Origin

This US breed allegedly traces its history back to 1620, and the landing of the *Mayflower* in what was to become America, when the breed's ancestors, English Cocker Spaniels, were brought by settlers. It was originally bred to flush and retrieve game birds – and would also happily take to the water.

USA

GREYHOUND

DOG

The fastest dog in the world, the GREYHOUND is able to reach speeds of over 64 km/h (40 mph), and throughout history, this canine athlete has been used for chasing and coursing all kinds of prey, although it has now become a racing animal. The very first races using an artificial lure took place near London in 1876 but it didn't catch on until the 1920s.

Features

The Greyhound is a strongly built but narrow dog with a long head, long, clean neck, deep chest, arched loin, powerful quarters and long, sound, muscular legs and feet. The fine, close coat can be black, white, red, blue, fawn, fallow, brindle or any of these broken with white.

Use

This breed is used as a companion dog and racing dog. Most companion dogs started life as part of the racing industry – although the show Greyhound is a very different animal. In early centuries, this breed was so prized that 'common folk' were not permitted to own one as only royalty and nobility could hunt with Greyhounds.

Similar breeds

Whippet, Sloughi

Height

Dog .... 71–76 cm (28–30 in)

Bitch ..... 69–71 cm (27–28 in)

Origin

This is an ancient English breed with a history that dates back longer than any other, having been depicted in art over 6,000 years ago. The name of this dog may come from the Anglo-Saxon word 'grei', which means beautiful, or it could just be a derivation of Great Hound.

England

BOSTON TERRIER

BITCH

The BOSTON TERRIER dates back to just after the American Civil War, and was developed in the murky world of dog-fighting and bull-baiting. It started as a cross between an English Bulldog and a White English Terrier, with later additions of French Bulldog to make the breed truer to type. It was first exhibited in 1888 and registered by the American Kennel Club in 1893.

Features

Though it is called a terrier, the Boston isn't a terrier at all. Its flat face, square head, big eyes, bat-like ears and smooth, short coat make this an eye-catching dog and, along with its compact size and short, smooth, easy-to-care-for coat, it is a very popular and stylish dog. The Boston Terrier can be either black or brindle with white markings.

Use

This friendly, good-natured breed makes an excellent companion – outgoing and social to all but especially affectionate and loyal to their owners. These active family dogs will get involved in all household activities, and are easy to train although prone to occasional bouts of stubbornness – and they snore!

Similar breeds

French Bulldog, Pug

Height

Dog .... 38–43 cm (15–17 in)

Bitch ..... 38–43 cm (15–17 in)

Origin

Sometimes called the 'American Gentleman', this is the first recorded genuinely US-bred dog originating, of course, in Boston, Massachusetts. The founding father of the breed, however, a dog called Hooper's Judge, was born in Liverpool, England and was shipped across the Atlantic in the 1870s.

USA

BICHON FRISÉ

BITCH

The Bichon Frisé was originally bred, possibly as far back as the thirteenth century, as a companion to the ladies of the Spanish nobility. These dogs were a frequent visitor to the courts of Spain and France from the sixteenth to the nineteenth centuries. They fell out of favour but their work as performing circus dogs kept the breed going, before it eventually returned to popularity in the late 1950s.

Features

Despite being small in size, the Bichon Frisé is a fairly sturdy, square little dog, with a fine, silky, white coat with corkscrew curls that require daily grooming to keep in good condition. In contrast, the eyes are dark and round with black rims and the nose is large, round, black and shiny. It should move effortlessly with a proud head carriage. The Bichon Frisé is always white.

Use

This is a good-natured, friendly, confident dog, which gets on with everyone in the family (including other dogs and cats) so makes an excellent companion dog. It is also clever, and so despite its size can often excel at training, obedience and agility.

Similar breeds

Bolognese, Maltese

Height

Dog .... 24–29 cm (9½–11½ in)

Bitch ..... 23–28 cm (9–11 in)

Origin

The Bichon Frisé was originally developed on the island of Tenerife, as a miniature version of an ancient Spanish water spaniel called the Barbet. The name Bichon comes from a contraction of Barbichon (little Barbet) and the breed was originally known as the Bichon Tenerife and later Bichon à Poil Frisé.

Spain

DOGUE DE BORDEAUX

BITCH

This powerful and muscular molossoid (mastiff-type) dog comes from France and was capable of defeating everything that stood in its way at least as far back as the seventeenth century. The DOGUE DE BORDEAUX was highly prized as a guardian, hunter and fighter, and was used to bait bulls, bears and wild cats as well as herd cattle and protect the homes of its master.

Features

The Dogue de Bordeaux is easily recognized from its massive head with prominent cheek muscles, oval eyes, small ears and stocky muscular body, which all give the impression of an imposing but also athletic dog. The skin of this breed is thick and loose fitting, and its fine, soft coat comes in all shades of fawn, sometimes as dark as mahogany, with white markings permissible on the chest. It can also have a darker coloured mask.

Use

Despite this breed's rather fearsome past, over the years and after almost total decline, the Dogue de Bordeaux has become smaller and far more amiable, making it an affectionate companion as well as still making an efficient guard dog if the need arises.

Similar breeds

Bullmastiff, Bulldog

Height

Dog .... 60–68 cm (23½–26¾ in)

Bitch ..... 57.5–66 cm (22¾– 26 in)

Origin

The history of this French breed is uncertain. There are many different theories, some linking the breed to the Tibetan Mastiff and others to the ancient dogs of Aquitaine. The breed is often known as the French Mastiff, although for a while in France it was known simply as the Dogue.

France

CANADIAN ESKIMO DOG

DOG

The CANADIAN ESKIMO DOG is an ancient sled-pulling dog that has been bred to have incredible strength and stamina for long-distance work rather than speed. Once common and widespread, it has survived as one of Canada's oldest breeds for over 4,000 years, but the introduction of snowmobiles and faster breeds have meant it is now rare.

Features

This is a typical spitz-type dog with a thick neck and a broad chest, well-boned legs and a majestic and powerful physique. It has short, thick, triangular ears, a level, well-muscled back, round feet with thick pads and hair between the toes, and a large, bushy tail carried over its back. The thick, dense coat can be any colour and have any markings.

Use

This is a breed that doesn't live easily as a pet as, despite being friendly and non-aggressive with people, it keeps its pack instincts so is mostly used as a sled dog and show dog. It is also designed for Arctic winters and not central heating. The breed has become more popular in Canada but there are few elsewhere.

Similar breeds

Siberian Husky, Alaskan Malamute

Height

Dog .... 64–69 cm (25–27 in)

Bitch ..... 53–61 cm (21–24 in)

Origin

Originating from Canada, this breed is sometimes called the American Husky, as a way of differentiating it from the Siberian Husky. Others call it the Inuit Sled Dog or the Canadian Inuit Dog but the northern people call it the Qimmiq or Kinmik. The breed has also been referred to as the 'Sherman'.

Canada

SWEDISH VALLHUND

BITCH

The Swedish name for the SWEDISH VALLHUND – Väsgötaspets – translates as 'Spitz Dog of the West Goths', while the name Vallhund simply means 'farm dog'. It was a multi-purpose farm dog, which was highly valued as it was strong enough to work as a heeler to move cattle herds in the Vastergotland in the south-west of Sweden, as well as act as a watchdog.

Features

The Swedish Vallhund is a small, sturdily built, long, low dog with pointed, pricked ears and oval, dark brown eyes giving it an alert expression. They may be born tailless. The Vallhund has a wolf-like coat that can be steel grey, greyish brown, greyish yellow, reddish yellow and reddish brown, with lighter hair of the same shade on the muzzle, throat, chest, belly, buttocks, feet and hocks. White markings are also acceptable.

Use

This is a companion breed – although some of these dogs have also proved to be successful in agility, flyball and obedience competitions. They make excellent family pets as they love children and are alert and energetic.

Similar breeds

Corgi, Lancashire Heeler

Height

Dog .... 33–35 cm (13–13¾ in)

Bitch ..... 30.5–33 cm (12–13 in)

Origin

The Swedish Vallhund is originally an old spitz-type breed that is believed to go back to the days of the Vikings. During the eighth century it seems that either these dogs were taken to Wales, or Welsh corgis were brought to Sweden, but interbreeding accounts for the many similarities between the two breeds.

Sweden

SHIH TZU

DOG

The name of this breed means 'Lion Dog' but it is often referred to as the 'Chrysanthemum Dog'. The SHIH TZU was a house pet for most of the Ming Dynasty in China, and was carried around in the wide sleeves of the court ladies. It was shown as the same breed as the Lhasa Apso until the Shih Tzu was registered as a separate breed in the 1940s.

Features

The original Chinese breed standard for the Shih Tzu must be the most romantic ever written. It says (among other things) that they should have the head of a lion, the face of an owl, the eyes of a dragon, the tongue of a peony petal, teeth like grains of rice, ears like palm leaves, the back of a tiger, the tail of a phoenix and the movement of a goldfish. As long as it fulfils those requirements, the Shih Tzu can be any colour!

Use

The Shih Tzu was, and still is, a companion dog. This is a happy, friendly, extrovert dog that loves life, and is equally at home tramping across the countryside as it is cuddling up as a lapdog.

Similar breeds

Lhasa Apso, Pekingese

Height

Dog .... 20–26.5 cm (8–10½ in)

Bitch ..... 20–25.5 cm (8–10 in)

Origin

Despite originating in China in the seventeenth century (or perhaps even earlier), the breed was hidden from the West until the twentieth century. It is thought to be a cross between resident Pekingese dogs and Lhasa Apsos that were brought as gifts to the courts of China from the great monasteries of Tibet.

China

ENGLISH SPRINGER SPANIEL

DOG

The English Springer Spaniel is a popular happy breed, whose tail never seems to stop wagging. The name comes from its original job, which was to make game 'spring up' and so be exposed to the hunter's guns. It was quickly realized that this was the perfect dog for tirelessly flushing game – able to push into the densest and thickest hedgerows and woodlands.

Features

This spaniel is a compact, strong, merry and active dog, with medium-sized, almond-shaped, kind eyes and long, wide ears set in line with its eyes. The coat is close, straight and weatherproof with feathering on its ears, forelegs, body and hindquarters. The colours of the coat can be liver and white, black and white, or either of these with tan markings.

Use

These dogs make great companions (with enough exercise) for an active family, friendly with everyone and able to join in with all family activities. The breed can excel in agility too. English Springer Spaniels are still very much used as working gun dogs for flushing and retrieving game.

Similar breeds

Field Spaniel, Cocker Spaniel

Height

Dog .... 51 cm (20 in)

Bitch ..... 48 cm (19 in)

Origin

Developed as a breed in the seventeenth century in England, this dog, the tallest of the British land spaniels, has changed little over the years, staying true to the original type. This spaniel breed, second only to the Cocker Spaniel in popularity, is very close to the original and now extinct Land Spaniel.

England

CHIHUAHUA

DOG

Despite being the smallest dog breed in the world, the CHIHUAHUA has a big personality. It comes in smooth-coated and, shown here, long-coated varieties, though many people think of them as a totally different breed, and indeed they are shown in separate classes. The first Chihuahuas were brought in to the USA from Mexico and were registered there in 1903.

Features

The Chihuahua has a characteristic dome-shaped skull, large eyes, level back and small, dainty feet with long, curved nails. If long-coated, the hair should be soft and either flat or slightly wavy with a plumed tail. If short-coated, it should be smooth and glossy with an undercoat and ruff allowed. The Chihuahua can be any colour or mixture except merle (dappled).

Use

Companion dog, but the breed has recently become popular as a celebrity fashion accessory – which isn't fair on either the dog, which is intelligent and trainable, or the people who meet it, because it can easily become a self-important guardian that is more than happy to use its tiny but surprisingly accurate teeth!

Similar breeds

Short-haired – Miniature Pinscher, Long-haired – Papillon

Height

Dog .... 15–20 cm (6–8 in)

Bitch ..... 15–20 cm (6–8 in)

Origin

Originating probably in Mexico, this breed was first encountered by Americans in the late nineteenth century but it may well be an ancient breed dating back to Aztec times, or it may have developed in Europe from the tiny comforter dogs of the Middle Ages. The long-coated version most likely came from the USA.

USA and Mexico

DACHSHUND (MINIATURE SHORT-HAIRED)
DOG

The DACHSHUND is, in personality, a cross between a hound and a terrier, and was originally bred in the 1600s to dig badgers and rabbits out of burrows. There are six different types of Dachshund – long-haired, wire-haired and smooth-haired, and also miniature long-haired, miniature wire-haired and miniature smooth-haired – but they all have the same characteristically long backs and short legs.

Features

This dog is low to the ground, with a long, straight body, short legs and a slightly curved tail. It has medium-sized, dark, almond-shaped eyes, broad, well-rounded ears and strong jaws. Despite its shape, which often leads to it being called a 'Sausage Dog', the body should be well clear of the ground so it can move freely with a long stride. Dachshunds can be any colour.

Use

The main use of the Dachshund is as a companion dog – although in the USA there are specific (and controversial) Dachshund racing (wiener racing) competitions. The miniature Dachshund is one of the most long-lived of all dog breeds.

Similar breeds

Miniature Long-Haired Dachshund, Miniature Wire-Haired Dachshund

Height

Dog .... 13–15 cm (5–6 in)

Bitch ..... 13–15 cm (5–6 in)

Origin

It is thought that a translation error explains why this breed appears in the hound group and not the terrier group. Originating in Germany, its name means 'Badger Dog', but in 1874, when the breed was entered in the English stud book, the German word 'hund' was incorrectly translated as 'hound' rather than 'dog'.

Germany

IRISH RED AND WHITE SETTER
BITCH

The Irish Red and White Setter is a breed in its own right, not just a different coloured Irish Setter. This is a dog that has been bred for the field since the seventeenth century, and is a strong, powerful, athletic dog with, supporters say, more brainpower and intelligence, than its purely red cousin – as well as being the older breed.

Features

A strong and athletic dog, this breed has a deep chest, powerful quarters and a strong, tapering tail. The coat, including its tail, is well feathered and finely textured, and the whole dog is more compact that its cousin the racy Irish (Red) Setter. It should be clearly parti-coloured – with a pearl white base colour and solid red patches on its head and body.

Use

This is an intelligent and endearing breed that makes a wonderful companion as long as it gets lots of exercise. The Irish Red and White Setter makes a great dog for an active family as its kind and friendly nature means it can get on with everybody. The breed is still also used as a working gun dog.

Similar breeds

Irish Setter, Gordon Setter

Height

Dog .... 66–74 cm (26–29 in)

Bitch ..... 64–71 cm (25–28 in)

Origin

This is the oldest of the Irish setters, although for some reason the least popular. This dog was originally bred in Ireland to work with birds of prey and was known as the Falconer's Dog for a while before guns became more advanced, at which time it became a gun dog.

Ireland

AKITA

DOG

Descended from the northern spitz dogs, the AKITA was refined into a specialist fighting dog in the seventeenth century in Japan. When dog-fighting fell out of favour, the breed found other work as a guard dog, a police dog, a hunting dog and as a companion. The breed first arrived in the USA in 1937 and it was registered with the Kennel Club in the same year.

Features

The largest of the Japanese breeds, the Akita is a powerful, muscular dog of the spitz type, and can be easily recognized by its size and almost bear-like coat, which is thick and coarse, with a soft, dense undercoat – and by the plush, bushy tail held over its back. It has dark brown, almond-shaped eyes, triangular ears and a large, broad head. The Akita can be any colour.

Use

Although used as companion dogs or sometimes guard dogs, they are best suited to experienced owners who understand the importance of training and socializing such a strong, stubborn and potentially highly territorial dog. Akitas are not an ideal family pet – mainly because they can be highly protective of 'their' children.

Similar breeds

Elkhound, Alaskan Malamute

Height

Dog .... 66–71 cm (26–28 in)

Bitch ..... 61–66 cm (24–26 in)

Origin

The Akita originates from Japan, where it is one of several breeds that have been classified as a national treasure. The breed's name comes from the rugged and mountainous Akita province on the northern end of Japan's Honsu island where the breed was first developed.

Japan

KEESHOND
BITCH

The KEESHOND, also known as the Dutch Barge Dog, descended from the same arctic ancestors as the Samoyed, Norwegian Elkhound and Finnish Spitz. These dogs originally served as watchdogs on riverboats and barges in the Dutch canals and rivers – and continue to be useful early warning systems to this day!

Features

The Keeshond is a typical spitz-type dog with a pointed muzzle, pricked, upright ears and almost ivy-shaped, dark eyes with black 'spectacles'. It has a thick, dense coat, which stands out away from its body and it has an impressive ruff. The tail is held up over its body often in a double curl. This breed comes in a rather wolfish mix of grey and black colours.

Use

This is an affectionate, good-natured dog who is outgoing and friendly with people and other dogs, and who is intelligent and learns quickly. It is mainly a companion dog now, although it can also act as a natural early warning system, alerting owners to the approach of strangers.

Similar breeds

Elkhound, Eurasier

Height

Dog .... 46 cm (18 in)

Bitch ..... 43 cm (17 in)

Origin

The eighteenth-century breed originates from Holland and takes its name from the Dutch patriot, Cornelius de Gyselaar who was nicknamed 'Kees'. The Keeshond became the symbol of the Dutch Patriot Party but the breed fell into decline at the same time as the Party did, almost dying out totally before eventually being re-established in the 1920s.

Holland

DALMATIAN
DOG

The earliest use of a DALMATIAN was recorded in England back in 1791; it was noted that the its unique appearance led to it being adopted as a high-status accompaniment to the carriages of the rich. The breed continued as a carriage dog until roads improved so much that they found it hard to keep up with carriages, and the motor car finally put an end to their livelihood.

Features

Dalmatians are the only dog breed that is truly spotted. They are strong, muscular dogs with a short, white coat with round and well-defined spots of either black or liver. If black spotted, they have a black nose, but if liver spotted, their nose will be brown. They should have a nicely arched neck, a smooth topline and a deep chest with plenty of heart and lung room. The legs are straight and strong with powerful hindquarters.

Use

An active family dog or competitive/show carriage dog, this breed's natural affinity for horses continues to this day. It originally ran alongside carriages to show the owners' high status, and on occasion to protect the travellers from highwaymen.

Similar breeds

In shape, Weimeraner, Hungarian Vizsla

Height

Dog .... 58–61 cm (23–24 in)

Bitch ..... 56–58 cm (22–23 in)

Origin

The ancestor of the Dalmatian is thought to be the now-extinct Talbot Hound, and despite the name, this English breed has no associations with the Dalmatian coast. This is one of the very few dogs developed for its looks rather than just its working ability – and also the only dog that was specifically bred as a carriage dog.

England

LABRADOR RETRIEVER

BITCH

The Labrador Retriever is the most popular breed of dog in the world. It is so versatile that this dog can be found doing a huge variety of jobs as well as its original task of retrieving game from the water – although it is probably as a Guide Dog and disability assistance dog that the breed has achieved the most respect and international acclaim.

Features

The Labrador has an ever-wagging, otter-like tail, soft, brown eyes, a clean-cut head and a short, smooth coat that comes in either yellow, black or chocolate colours. It moves effortlessly and always looks happy – as much a feature of the breed as its appearance.

Use

This breed has many uses including companion dog, disability assistance dog and gun dog. Their good nature and ability to get on with children make Labradors a very popular family dog. However, these dogs are bred to work all day every day, and are also very greedy so the combination of lack of exercise and too much food can lead to many Labradors being overweight.

Similar breeds

Golden Retriever, Flat-coated Retriever

Height

Dog .... 56–57 cm (22–22½ in)

Bitch ..... 55–56 cm (21½–22 in)

Origin

While many people think of the Labrador Retriever as being a British breed, it was originally bred to work alongside the fishermen of Newfoundland, Canada, to pull in nets and catch escaping fish. After being crossed with setters and other retrievers, the breed developed into the perfect retrieving gun dog. Despite that, these dogs still maintain their love of water.

Canada

GREAT DANE

DOG

The GREAT DANE holds the record for being the tallest dog breed in the world. Although in its present form it has only worked as a guard dog, the ancestors of this canine colossus have been war dogs, fighting dogs and high-status hunting dogs. They are now gentle giants, bred for their docility – their deep, powerful bark being far worse then their largely non-existent bite.

Features

A giant, muscular, strong, elegant dog with a high head and neck carriage, the Great Dane has an alert, majestic bearing. It has a large, strong head, deep set, round eyes, and medium-sized, triangular ears. The long legs are also strong and muscular, giving it strength and galloping power. The breed has a short, dense, sleek coat that can come in brindle, fawn, blue, black and harlequin.

Use

The Great Dane is a companion dog but needs a very special owner, as despite its good nature, nothing is out of reach for such a tall dog. It is often said that the greatest threat from this dog is that it will eat you out of house and home!

Similar breeds

Irish Wolfhound, Deerhound

Height

Dog .... 76 cm (30 in)

Bitch ..... 71 cm (28 in)

Origin

Originally this was a high-status dog of the hunting field before being bred to be larger and finer. Despite the name, this is a German dog and not a Danish one. In fact in 1876, the breed was declared the National Dog of Germany. It has also been known as the German Mastiff and the Deutsche Dogge.

Germany

FIELD SPANIEL

DOG

This is one of the rarer spaniels and is a medium-sized flushing dog, developed originally as a working gun dog that could find, flush and retrieve anything with fur or feathers. The FIELD SPANIEL was particularly good at activity and endurance in heavy cover, over difficult terrain and in water. However, in the mid nineteenth century the breed became more a show dog than a worker.

Features

This is a well-balanced spaniel that should look like it could easily do a day's work. It has a typical spaniel head with gentle, dark eyes, and long, wide, feathered ears. The Field Spaniel coat is long, flat, silky and dense, and has abundant feathering on the chest, under the body and behind the legs and tail. The coat can be black, liver or roan, or any of these with tan markings.

Use

The Field Spaniel is said to be one of the most docile of the spaniels and is a fun-loving companion so makes a fabulous family dog for those living in the country who can give it the exercise required. It is still used as a working gun dog.

Similar breeds

Springer Spaniel, Cocker Spaniel

Height

Dog .... 46 cm (18 in)

Bitch ..... 46 cm (18 in)

Origin

This breed originated in England in the mid 1800s but it fell out of favour. Its future seemed bleak until the 1960s when enthusiasts decided to try and save the breed and bring it back to its working origins instead of the show dog it had become. By using Cocker and Springer Spaniel crosses, the breed's future now seems to be secure.

England

POMERANIAN

BITCH

The Pomeranian was developed through selective breeding from the larger spitz breeds. It was introduced into the UK by Queen Charlotte. Her husband, King George III, was from Meckenberg, which borders Pomerania, the north-east corner of East Germany. Later, her granddaughter, Queen Victoria, made these outgoing dogs fashionable in England, and even showed them at Crufts in 1891.

Features

Although the smallest of the spitz breeds, the Pomeranian has the same characteristic appearance, with a compact body, long, straight topcoat and smooth, fluffy undercoat. It also has the typical huge ruff, foxy face and fluffy, plumed tail held over its back. It can be any colour and often resembles a ball of fluff!

Use

Pomeranians are much-loved companion dogs – although some compete in mini-agility. Their small size and endearing looks combined with big personalities and docile temperament make them excellent pets.

Similar breeds

German Spitz, Finnish Spitz

Height

Dog .... 18–20 cm (7–8 in)

Bitch ..... 18–20 cm (7–8 in)

Origin

This breed is originally from the historic area of Pomerania that is now present-day Germany and Poland. The spitz breeds that this dog descends from, however, are the sled dogs and herding dogs of Iceland and Lapland – which explains why it has such a thick, abundant coat.

Germany and Poland

CARDIGAN WELSH CORGI

DOG

There are two types of Corgi – the CARDIGAN WELSH CORGI and the Pembroke Welsh Corgi. The breeds are very similar – in fact it wasn't until 1927 that they were shown at Crufts as separate breeds. Despite being a small dog, the Corgi was used for moving cattle and, like all heelers, did this by nipping at their heels.

Features

The Corgi is a low-set, heavy-boned dog with a deep chest and upright ears. The main difference between the two Corgis is that the Cardigan has a long, bushy tail and larger, rounded ears. They are also darker in colour and slightly larger, heavier and longer. The Cardigan Welsh Corgi has also been called the Yard Dog – because it was said it was a Welsh yard between the tip of its nose to the tip of its tail. The breed can be any colour.

Use

This is a companion dog but as a 'one-man breed' it needs socializing with as many people and dogs as possible, as it can be reserved with strangers and utterly fearless when faced with much larger dogs.

Similar breeds

Pembroke Welsh Corgi, Swedish Vallhund

Height

Dog .... 29–32 cm (11½–12½ in)

Bitch ..... 26.5–29 cm (10½–11½ in)

Origin

Originating in Wales, 'corgi' derives from the Celtic word for dog. The Cardigan Welsh Corgi is the older of the two breeds, and arrived in Cardiganshire with the Celts as far back as 1200 BC. The Cardigan Welsh Corgi is also far rarer – so much so that it is included on the UK Vulnerable Native Breed list.

Wales

CHESAPEAKE BAY RETRIEVER

BITCH

Of all the water-retrieval dogs, the CHESAPEAKE BAY RETRIEVER is probably the toughest. It was developed to be equally at home in the water as it is on land, and so has a weatherproof coat that allows it to hunt waterfowl in rough and icy waters. This breed is totally tireless and can easily retrieve several hundred birds a day.

Features

This is a well-proportioned, muscular dog, looking similar in appearance to a Labrador but larger. It is meant to blend into its surroundings and so the colours permitted are dead grass (straw to bracken), sedge (red gold), and any shade of brown or ash. The Chesapeake has a distinctive, oily, double coat, which resists water and allows it to work in adverse weather conditions including ice and snow.

Use

Chesapeakes are happy dogs whose love of life, and love of water means that they make great companions for an outdoor active family. As working retrievers or for trials, they have huge stamina and can work all day. They are very devoted and totally loyal to their owner's family.

Similar breeds

Labrador Retriever, Curly-coated Retriever

Height

Dog .... 58–66 cm (23–26 in)

Bitch ...... 53–61 cm (21–24 in)

Origin

It is thought that this breed dates back to the shipwreck of an English brig off the coast of Maryland, USA in 1807, from which two Newfoundlands were rescued. These were bred to local retrievers, along with the English Otterhound, Flat-coated Retriever and the Curly-coated Retriever. The Chesapeake Bay Retriever was the result.

USA

BOUVIER DES FLANDERS
DOG

The Bouvier des Flanders originated as a farm dog, descending from the Tibetan Mastiff, Schnauzer and Beuceron among others. The breed worked both as a guardian and also as a cattle herder. Early breeders were far more interested in working ability than looks, and while the dog had been known in its native land for centuries, the first breed standard wasn't drawn up until 1912.

Features

While the Bouvier des Flanders isn't a common breed, once seen it is never forgotten as such a large, imposing, strong dog with a thick, coarse, curly coat and a formidable beard definitely makes a lasting impression. It has a compact, powerful body, a strong, muscled neck and may be born tailless. The Bouvier can be black, brindle or fawn – although in the USA, it can be any colour.

Use

This is, without doubt, not a dog for everyone, although it is used as a companion dog, service dog and guard dog. The Bouvier is fiercely loyal to its family, while often being problematical with strangers – both people and dogs.

Similar breeds

Russian Black Terrier, Giant Schnauzer

Height

Dog .... 62–70 cm (24½–27½ in)

Bitch ..... 60–68 cm (23½–26½ in)

Origin

This Belgian breed takes its name from the area that now includes parts of Belgium, France and Holland, where it was most popular. It was very nearly decimated in the First World War, but found work as a messenger dog and ambulance dog, and was later re-established by a Belgian vet.

Belgium

CHINESE CRESTED
BITCH

The CHINESE CRESTED is a fine-boned, elegant toy dog that turns heads with its appearance. There are two varieties; the hairless variety's skin is warm and soft to the touch – something that has given rise to all kinds of myths. In England in the early 1900s, for example, it was known as the 'fever dog' as it was thought that touching the skin of this dog would cure certain ailments!

Features

The Chinese Crested can be one of two types – the Deer type, which is racy and fine boned, or the Cobby type with is heavier in bone and body. They also come in two coat varieties – the Hairless, which has soft, silky hair only on its crest, tail and feet, and the Powderpuff (shown here), which is covered with a double, soft, straight coat. They can be any colour or combination of colours.

Use

This dog is very much a companion dog, though some can excel at mini-agility. The advantages of the hairless breed are that it has no body odour, no shedding and is less likely to cause allergies but it does need to be kept warm in winter and protected from the sun in summer.

Similar breeds

Mexican Hairless

Height

Dog .... 28–33 cm (11–13 in)

Bitch ..... 23–30.5 cm (9–12 in)

Origin

While this breed is acknowledged to come from China, its origins are actually fairly uncertain. Hairless breeds probably started out in Africa before being traded among merchants and heading east to Asia where they became popular. Visitors to China were fascinated by these naked dogs, and in turn brought them back to Europe for their novelty value.

China

KOMONDOR
DOG

Komondors are a large, muscular breed known for their corded coat that makes them look rather like an enormous mop. The coat protects them from the weather and attacks from predators. The dogs were used for flock guarding and were raised with their flocks so that they bonded strongly to them and would protect them from wolves, bears or even human predators.

Features

This is a large, imposing dog with plenty of bone and strength. The Komondor has a large head with almond-shaped, dark brown eyes and elongated, triangular ears. Its back is level and strong and it is slightly longer than it is high. Its most striking feature, however, is its long, corded coat, which forms naturally and is always white so it can blend in with the sheep.

Use

These dogs were bred to take care of their flock without human help,.so they tend to think for themselves, which can make training tricky! They are highly intelligent, intensely loyal and devoted, and enjoy physical contact so make good companion dogs. In their native Hungary, they are still used as flock guards.

Similar breeds

Bergamasco, Hungarian Puli

Height

Dog .... 70 cm (27¾ in)

Bitch ..... 65 cm (25½ in)

Origin

This is an ancient breed thought to have arrived in Hungary with the Mongols in the thirteenth century. It was developed as one of three working breeds– with the Puli herding the sheep and the Komondor and the Kuvasz guarding them. The Komondor is a direct descendant of the Aftscharka, a breed founded by nomadic tribes as they swept through Russia.

Hungary

HOVAWART
DOG

The Hovawart takes its name from the early German for farm or estate ('hof') and watch or guard ('wart') – illustrating that the breed was the guardian of the estate. This was a job it did for centuries, and continues to do so, protecting the livestock and courtyards of German farms. It is a new breed to the show ring but is a very rare dog indeed.

Features

This powerful, medium-sized dog is slightly longer than it is high. It has a well-balanced body, strong, deep chest, powerful hindquarters and a bushy tail that is raised over its back when it is alert or moving. The Hovawart has a long, weatherproof, dense coat that is shorter on the head and front of the legs, and it can be black, black and gold, or blonde.

Use

The breed is known for being patient, reliable, intelligent and responsive, and so if Hovawarts existed in greater numbers, they would doubtless make their presence felt in most of the dog sports as well as being just a show dog, companion dog and farm dog in their native land.

Similar breeds

Golden Retriever, Flat-coated Retriever

Height

Dog .... 64–70 cm (25–27½ in)

Bitch ..... 58–65 cm (23–25½ in)

Origin

This German breed dates back to the 1200s, and in the Middle Ages it was a legendary farm guard but the breed fell into virtual total decline. In the 1920s it was redeveloped although there is some argument as to whether it is true to the original breed – but it certainly looks the part.

Germany

KING CHARLES SPANIEL

BITCH

The KING CHARLES SPANIEL takes its name from King Charles II of England, who was an enthusiastic breeder of these miniature spaniels – in fact it was said that for a while Hampton Court Palace was 'over-run with these dogs'. While he may have popularized the breed, there were dwarf spaniels in England long before his reign.

Features

The King Charles Spaniel is one of the largest toy breeds – but still has the distinctive spaniel appearance. It is a refined, compact and cobby dog with a domed head, large, dark, appealing eyes, a short, turned-up nose and long, well-feathered ears. Its back is short and level and the tail is well-feathered. The long, silky, straight coat can come in black and tan, tricolour, Blenheim or ruby varieties.

Use

In some ways this is an ideal urban dog – friendly, happy, intelligent, trainable and affectionate, and so makes a wonderful family companion dog. Some also enjoy work as pets as therapy dogs and can do well in obedience classes.

Similar breeds

Cavalier King Charles Spaniel, Tibetan Spaniel

Height

Dog .... 28–30.5 cm (11–12 in)

Bitch ..... 25.5–28 cm (10–11 in)

Origin

Originating in England, these dogs were bred to become smaller and more flat-faced during the Victorian era. In the 1920s, efforts were made to return the breed to its original form by breeding larger, longer-nosed dogs. Eventually the two different types split into the King Charles Spaniel and the newer Cavalier King Charles Spaniel.

England

LÖWCHEN

BITCH

The Löwchen (or Little Lion Dog) is an old but still rare breed that started life over 400 years ago as a court dog in pre-Renaissance Europe. The distinctive clip, where the coat on the hindquarters is totally removed apart from cuffs left on the ankles, was both to highlight the breed's resemblance to a lion, but also so ladies could warm their feet on the exposed skin.

Features

In the show ring, the 'lion' clip easily identifies the breed, as it is always shown clipped. The hair that remains is long, silky and wavy but never curly. The Löwchen also has a strong, short body, a proudly arched neck and a plumed tail that is carried jauntily over its body when it moves. The eyes are rounded, set well apart and should be as dark as possible, with an expression of kindness and intelligence. All colours and markings are acceptable in this breed.

Use

While making fabulous companions, these are intelligent, quick, little dogs, and they are beginning to make their presence felt in sports such as mini-agility, heelwork to music and obedience.

Similar breeds

Maltese, Havanese

Height

Dog .... 30.5–35.5 cm (12–14 in)

Bitch ..... 25.5–30.5 cm (10–12 in)

Origin

It is thought that the Löwchen developed as a distinct breed from a breeding colony in Lyon in the south of France – despite the German name, which means 'little lion'. The breed virtually died out in the 1900s and was considered the world's rarest dog before being re-established by Madame Bennert of Brussels who is credited as being its saviour.

France

REPORTAGE

The REWARDING PARTNERSHIP between *man* and his '*best friend*' has clearly passed with FLYING COLOURS. Indeed, there's *no bone of contention* – it's as worthy of a ROSETTE as the *agile* and *athletic, handsome* and *huggable dogs* in these wonderful behind-the-scenes photographs. The book's final pages certainly have a *wag or two in their tail.*

Discover Dogs,
Earls Court,
London, UK

I know I'm only short but can I have a treat too?

I've been collared by the photographer again

Oh, fur goodness sake, stop complaining. Did he get my best side?

Excuse me. I think you'll find I'm much more beautiful.

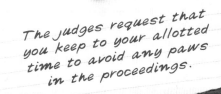

The judges request that you keep to your allotted time to avoid any paws in the proceedings.

I'm having a
bad hair day

I'm a wash-and-go
kind of dog myself

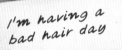

• Hearing Dogs f
• Support Dogs

Dog grooming tool kit

- ☑ combs
- ☑ brushes
- ☑ clippers
- ☑ scissors
- ☑ nail trimmers
- ☑ shampoo
- ☑ conditioner
- ☑ hairdryer

It's all about speed, agility and dogged determination. It's a dog beat dog world out there at Earls Court...

Chin up, guys! We can't all be as beautiful as me.

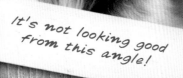

It's not looking good from this angle!

Every dog has its day and this is ours.

This is one
hair-raising
day

Third place wasn't
bad was it?

Go on, read my name
out. . . please.

GLOSSARY

Action the way a dog moves

Agility a sport where dogs have to negotiate a variety of obstacles including jumps and tunnels

Assistance dog a dog trained to help owners with disabilities

Bitch a female dog

Brindle a coat patterned with streaks of darker or black markings

Brisket the sternum, or in some breeds, the entire thorax

Canidae the family of carnivores that the dog belongs to

Cat feet small, rounded, compact feet

Cobby stocky, square body

Corded hair that is formed into carefully constructed matts or dreadlocks

Corkscrew tail a twisted tail

Croup the part of the back stretching from the root of the tail up to just above the hips

Dewclaw a fifth claw on the inside of the leg (a few breeds have double dewclaws)

Dog any canine, or specifically a male

Double-coated a warm, thick undercoat that is resistant to wet and cold, and then a more weatherproof topcoat

Drop ear a folding ear

Feathering long hair on the back of the legs and tail

Flank the side of a dog's body between the last rib and the hip

Flushing driving game from cover

Gait the pattern of leg movements in different paces

Gay tail a tail that is held up over the back

Guard hairs long, thick hairs that create the top coat

Gun dog a group of dogs developed to assist hunters in finding and retrieving game

Grizzle white hairs running through darker hairs

Liver a coat colour of brown

Heeler a dog that moves herds of cattle by nipping at their heels

Height the measurement from the ground to a dog's withers (same as a horse)

Lurcher a sight hound cross, usually intentionally bred, and originally used as a poacher's dog

Mastiff one of several breeds of large, powerful, short-haired dogs (also known as Molossoid)

Muzzle the part of the head in front of the eyes

Pedigree the record of a dog's ancestry

Pied a coat that has patches of white with another colour

Pinscher German for 'terrier' (or 'biter')

Pointing the action of freezing and indicating the position of game

Prick ear a pointed, erect ear

Purebred a dog that has parents both belonging to the same breed

Racy a dog that shows racing lines rather than heavier lines

Ruff a mane of hair around the neck like a lion's

Sable hairs of one colour that are tipped with black

Scent hound a hound that hunts using their sense of smell to follow a trail

Setting the action of freezing on sight of game and then flushing it out on command

Sight hound a hound that hunts using its keen eyesight

Spitz one of several breeds of heavy-coated, stocky dogs of northern European origin characterized by erect ears and a heavily coated tail carried over the back

Stop the depression between the skull and the muzzle

Tail set the position of the tail

Thick-set a broad and solid dog

Topline the outline of the top of a dog's body

Tucked up small-waisted compared to the chest, or when the body has a shallow depth at the loin

Water dog a dog bred to retrieve from water

Wheaten the colour of wheat

Withers the highest point on the dog's back, just behind the neck

Underline the outline of the underneath of the dog's body

SHOWS

BRITAIN
Crufts Dog Show
(contact Kennel Club, see right)
www.crufts.org.uk

Discover Dogs
(contact Kennel Club, see right)
www.discoverdogs.org.uk

USA
AKC/Eukanuba National Championship
(contact American Kennel Club, see right)
classic.akc.org/invitational

National Dog Show
The Kennel Club of Philadelphia
nds.nationaldogshow.com

Westminster Dog Show
The Westminster Kennel Club
149 Madison Avenue, Suite 402
New York, NY 10016
USA
Tel: 01 212 213 3165
www.westminsterkennelclub.org

INTERNATIONAL SHOWS
FCI Dog Show Portal
www.eurodogshow.info

The FCI organizes the following shows; their location and contact details change annually:

World Dog Show

European Section Show

The Americas and the Caribbean Section Show

Asia and the Pacific Section Show

ASSOCIATIONS
BRITAIN
The Kennel Club
1–5 Clarges Street
London W1J 8AB
UK
Tel: 0044 844 463 3980
www.the-kennel-club.org.uk

CANADA
Canadian Kennel Club
200 Ronson Drive
Suite 400
Etobicoke
Ontario M9W 5Z9
Canada
Tel: 01 416 675 5511
www.ckc.ca

USA
American Kennel Club
8051 Arco Corporate Drive
Suite 100
Raleigh
NC 27617-3390
USA
Tel: 01 919 233 9767
www.akc.org

INTERNATIONAL
Federation Cynologique International
FCI Office
Place Albert 1er, 13
B-6530, Thuin
Belgium
www.fci.be

The FCI is a federation of 87 national organizations, including the following:

AUSTRALIA
Australian National Kennel Club
P.O. Box 309
Carina
Queensland 4152
Australia
Tel: 0061 7 3398 8608
www.ankc.org.au

BELGIUM
Societe Royale Saint-Hubert
98 Avenue Albert Giraud
B-1030, Bruxelles
Belgium
Tel: 0032 2 245 4840
www.srsh.be

DENMARK
Dansk Kennel Klub
Parkvej 1
2680 Solrød Strand
Denmark
Tel: 0045 56 188100
www.dansk-kennel-klub.dk

FINLAND
Suomen Kennelliitto-Finska Kennelklubben
Kamreerintie 8
SF 02770
Espoo
Finland
Tel: 00358 9887300
www.kennelliitto.fi

FRANCE
Société Centrale Canine
155, avenue Jean Jaurès
F93535 Aubervilliers Cedex
France
Tel: 0033 1 49 37 54 00
www.scc.asso.fr

GERMANY
Verband für das Deutsche Hundewesen
Westfalendamm 174
44141 Dortmund
Germany
Tel: 0049 231/565 000
www.vdh.de

INDIA
Kennel Club of India
No. 28/89, AA Block
First Street, Anna Nagar
Chennai 600 040
India
Tel: 0091 44 26213661
www.thekci.org

ITALY
Ente Nazionale della Cinofilia Italiane
Via Le Corsica 20
20137, Milan
Italy
Tel: 0039 027002031
www.enci.it

NETHERLANDS
Dutch Kennel Club
De Raad van Beheer op Kynologisch gebied in Nederland
Postbus 75901
1070 AX Amsterdam
Netherlands
Tel: 0031 20 664 471
www.kennelclub.nl

NEW ZEALAND
New Zealand Kennel Club
Prosser Street
Private Bag 50903
Porirua 5240
New Zealand
Tel: 0064 4 237 4489
www.nzkc.org.nz

PORTUGAL
Clube Portugues de Canicultura
Rue Frei Carlos 7
1600-095 Lisbon
Portugal
Tel: 00351 217 994 790
www.cpc.pt

SINGAPORE
The Singapore Kennel Club
170 Upper Bukit Timah Road
Suite 12-02
Bukit-Timah Shopping Centre
Singapore 588179
Tel: 0065 469 4821
www.skc.org.sg

SOUTH AFRICA
Kennel Union of Southern Africa
P.O. Box 2659
Cape Town 8000
South Africa
Tel: 0027 21 423 9027
www.kusa.co.za

SOUTH KOREA
Korea Kennel Federation
5F, #252-23
Yongdu-dong
Dongdaemun-gu
Seoul
Korea
Tel: 0082 22278
www.thekkf.or.kr

SPAIN
Real Sociedad Canina de Espana
C Lagasca 16
28001, Madrid
Spain
Tel: 0034 914 264960
www.rsce.es

SWEDEN
Svenska Kennelklubben
SE-163 85 Spanga
Sweden
Tel: 0046 8 795 3000
www.skk.se

SWITZERLAND
Societe Cynologique Suisse
Brunnmattstrasse 24
3007 Berne
Switzerland
Tel: 0041 3130 66262
www.skg.ch

PICTURE CREDITS

iStockphoto/Zeljko Santrac (p7); Getty Images/ Steve Baccon (p8); iStockPhoto/Mike Dabell (p9); iStockPhoto/ Robert Churchill (p10); Getty Images/Hulton Archive/H. William Tetlow (p11); Getty Images/AFP/ Ian Kington (p12) and Fotolia/ Richard Paul (p13).

PUBLISHER'S ACKNOWLEDGEMENTS

We would like to thank the organizers of Discover Dogs, Beate Rothon from Markus-Mühle and Emily Owen for their help with the photoshoot.

We would like to thank all of the following dog owners and breeders who allowed us to photograph their dogs for this book.

Afghan Hound Mr and Mrs King
Akita Paula Donnelly
Alaskan Malamute Charlotte John
American Cocker Spaniel Margaret Hatley
Bedlington Terrier Chris Harris
Bichon Frisé Ann Toogood
Bolognese Andrew Hollis
Boston Terrier Jo King
Bouvier des Flanders Janet Garrett
Canadian Eskimo Dog Elizabeth Salter
Cardigan Welsh Corgi Emily Day
Chesapeake Bay Retriever Wyn Thomas
Chihuahua Sue Lee
Chinese Crested Sharon and Shannon Roberts
Dachshund (Miniature Short-Haired) Sue Ergis
Dalmatian Kerry Harrison-Stratford
Dogue de Bordeaux Debbie Rainger
English Springer Spaniel Judith Andrew
Field Spaniel Chloe Aifrey
Foxhound Jackie Wallace
French Bulldog Patricia Glassey
German Shepherd Dog Patricia Glassey
German Spitz Lynda Hewett
Golden Retriever Norman Austin
Great Dane Sharon Rose
Greyhound Anne Ball
Griffon Bruxellois Ade Akilaja
Hovawart Mrs K Woodger
Hungarian Puli Mrs E Reid
Irish Red and White Setter Mr R Knapton
Keeshond Jane Saunders
King Charles Spaniel Christine Dix
Komondor Anita and Gary Waters
Labrador Retriever Alison Scutcher
Löwchen Steve Beall
Manchester Terrier Judy Thurlow
Norfolk Terrier Linda Philip
Papillon Shane Small
Pointer Jan Risbridger
Pomeranian Sarah Parker
Shih Tzu Debbie Willett
Staffordshire Bull Terrier Jo-Ann Essex
Swedish Vallhund Sue Hodkinson

111

INDEX